Layout and design by Meghan Cully.

This book may be purchased for business or promotional use or for special sales.

Oopsie Daisy

DEDICATION

To all the blind/visually impaired dogs saved by the Blind Dog Rescue Alliance (BDRA)
who showed me the true meaning of "Blind dogs see with their hearts."

To all the BDRA volunteers who work tirelessly to save these sweet souls,
and to all the wonderful adopters who open their homes to these pups.

And finally, to my special girl, Oopsie Daisy, who is an inspiration and joy every single day.

Howdy! I'm Oopsie
Daisy and this is my story.

Oopsie Daisy is a very special Australian
Shepherd (Aussie for short) puppy.

When Oopsie was born her dog mommy noticed something special about her.

She was not like the other pups. Oopsie could only see out of one eye, and she was deaf, meaning she couldn't hear anything.

The breeder who owned all the dogs said Oopsie was not perfect, so he would not be able to sell her.

Oopsie's dog mommy did not care that her baby was deaf and partially blind. She loved her very much as she was and just knew that she could find a good home.

Oopsie could not hear "I love you" from her dog mommy, but she could feel how much she was loved by lots of kisses and cuddles.

The other pups knew their sister was different, and they would tease her by sneaking up to scare her.

At first, Oopsie was scared and unhappy with being picked on.

Don't tease me.
You scare me

But she didn't let it get her down for long.

Oopsie decided to show the other pups that she could do anything they did, and more.

See, I can play just like all of you.

She showed everyone how she could be happy and run and play and fetch just like them. And more than the other puppies, Oopsie spread happiness to everyone around her.

As the weeks went by, all of the pups were adopted one by one. They left for their new homes to be happy and loved.

No one wanted a deaf and almost blind dog, because they thought being a parent to Oopsie would be hard work. Oopsie promised herself that she would be happy no matter what.

This one is no good. She is deaf and can't see from one eye.

Then one day a lady came who wanted to take Oopsie home.

Oopsie was SO happy she finally had a person to love her and to give her a home of her own.

But happiness in the new home did not last very long.

The day came that her new family did not have enough time to take care of Oopsie.

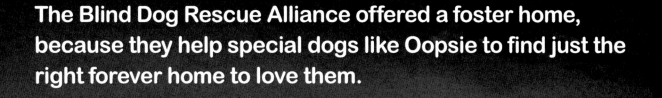

The Blind Dog Rescue Alliance offered a foster home, because they help special dogs like Oopsie to find just the right forever home to love them.

Oopsie came to her new foster home and instantly fell in love with her human foster mommy, dog foster brother, a Siberian Husky named Juno, and one foster sister named Gretchen.

Within a short time, Oopsie's foster mommy and siblings fell in love with her. Her mommy really enjoyed watching Oopsie play and fetch and going for runs with her.

Oopsie was so happy in this home and made her foster mommy and siblings so happy that her foster mommy decided to adopt her.

Oopsie loves her new mommy very much and is grateful that her mommy loves her enough to play with her and to teach her good manners.

I love my
new family!

Oopsie is a very smart little girl, but since she is deaf, she cannot hear when her mommy talks to her.

So, Oopsie's mommy teaches her hand signs. She knows sit and down.

Watch me! I can do these commands. I'm sitting and staying.

Sit

She also knows to come inside when her mommy flashes the porch light off and on.

Down

She also loves her stuffed toys. She cannot hear the squeaking, but she still loves to tear open the toys to find the squeaker.

Oopsie treats all pups the same and helps other dogs who cannot see or hear well.

Hello, puppy. Don't be afraid. I will be your friend and play with you.

She even shares her favorite stuffed toys with new foster dogs to make them feel safe and welcome when they are sick or scared.

Here is my favorite toy to make you feel better.

Oopsie also loves to play with kids.

Let's play fetch!

Because her life is so special, Oopsie helps the Blind Dog Rescue Alliance show everyone that blind and deaf dogs can have very happy lives, just like seeing and hearing dogs.

She goes to events to educate people about how to live with a dog that has special needs and to help other dogs find homes.

Blind Dog Rescue Alliance
Blind dogs see with their hearts

www.blinddogrescue.com

Oopsie Daisy is a ray of sunshine and brings joy to every day!

Blind dogs really do see with their hearts.

Proceeds from the sale of this book will go to the Blind Dog Rescue Alliance (BDRA).

BDRA is a 501(c)3 non-profit organization. It is a 100% volunteer-based organization made up of over 100 volunteers from across the United States and Eastern Canada.

The mission of BDRA is to rescue dogs that are either blind or visually impaired, because although blind dogs can and do lead full and happy lives, they have a very limited amount of time in a shelter as they are considered to have low adoption potential.

Once BDRA is made aware of potential dogs for rescue, the dogs are pulled from shelters and placed into foster care where their health and other potential issues can be evaluated and addressed before being placed for adoption. In its first 10 years, since forming in 2009, BDRA has rescued over 650+ dogs and has paid more than $200,000 in veterinarian bills. All BDRA funds come from the generous donations of supporters.

Please look over the BDRA website (**www.blinddogrescue.org**), visit the blind dogs for adoption, and read their stories. I think you will agree that "Blind Dogs See With Their Hearts!"

If you want to help other dogs like Oopsie and her friends find their forever homes, reach out to your local animal shelter or rescue. They are always in need of volunteers and adopters!

This book is brought to you by the following

Oopsie Daisy

The real Oopsie Daisy is an Australian Shepherd. She was born in Pennsylvania, adopted from the internet, and then surrendered to Blind Dog Rescue Alliance. She was fostered by Deb Marsh, who immediately fell in love with Oopsie and her contagious smile. Deb soon "foster failed" and adopted Oopsie.

Deborah Marsh

Deb Marsh is a US Air Force veteran who lives in York, Pennsylvania with her family of adopted BDRA dogs. Deb has been a volunteer with the Blind Dog Rescue Alliance for over eight years and has fostered many dogs in that time.

Shelagh Cully

Shelagh Cully is a local published illustrator based near Baltimore, Maryland. Her work often focuses on female representations in contemporary media, and animal welfare. See more of Shelagh's work at @artbyshelagh on instagram and facebook.

Can you draw your favorite pet or animal?

Made in the USA
Middletown, DE
12 April 2020